# Contents

# Introduction

The single most distinctive characteristic of worship in the late twentieth century is "contemporary Christian music." The advent of new instruments, new tunes, and new texts is transforming worship for the new millennium. The songs are personal and corporate, enthusiastic and reflective, Christocentric and Spirit-filled. This book introduces mainline congregations to this new chorus music.

The *Chorus Book* has been prepared to serve all those who like to sing in church especially "young Christians." Like the African American spirituals, camp meeting refrains, nineteenth-century gospel hymns, and Hispanic corritos, this book reflects the heart rhythms and language of our people.

The *Chorus Book* complements the traditional worship of congregations by being a supplement to, not a replacement of, excellent hymnals and worship resources. Traditional hymns, because of their depth and richness, will continue in many congregations to be the bedrock of congregational singing. The inclusion of a number of traditional refrains and selections from hymnals and books of worship indicates indebtedness to traditional music. Many congregations, however, now desire to explore and use a new range of music, and we hope they will add this book to their hymnal rack.

What is distinctive about this volume? The book's outline follows the basic pattern of worship found in many mainline congregations, a pattern often described as "Word and Table." It includes choruses for baptism and holy communion, as well as choruses for popular new liturgies such as healing and daily prayer services. The selection includes some of the most popular Christian choruses in the United States and Canada today. The language is thoroughly modern, using inclusive language for persons and biblical language for God wherever permitted. Reflecting God's rainbow church, African Americans, Asians, Hispanics, and persons from around the world have all contributed to the collection. To encourage the use of contemporary instruments, every song includes guitar chords. Exceptionally extensive indexes will help worship planners select music appropriate to scripture, topic, Christian year, and location in worship.

The editors are practitioners of this new music, but still learners. We offer what we now know, but recognize that we still have much to discover. We welcome your critique and suggestions for new material in subsequent volumes. We offer this book to singing congregations with the hope that through our music, both traditional and modern, God may be glorified.

Pentecost 1996
J. Michael Bryan, M. Anne Burnette Hook, Andy Langford, Brian McSwain

# How to Use Choruses in Worship

Y ou are holding a brand new worship resource for "mainline" or "traditional" churches. The *Chorus Book* brings a whole new genre of music to the hearts, hands, and voices of worshipers. God's people are singing people. Throughout history, we have sung to hear God's Word and God's call to us; we have also sung as a response to God's call to us and love for us. Our songs affirm our faith; they also help us ask our questions. Through singing we pray for the Spirit to be present in our worship and in our lives, and we rejoice in God's presence with and in us.

The *Chorus Book* enables us to continue this rich tradition of singing. The choruses in this book will help a new generation of Christians to worship in their own "heart language." As God continues to reach out to us, we can reach out to God and worship God "in spirit and in truth." Singing helps us to express our love for God with all our heart, mind, soul, and strength.

**What Is the Point of This Book?** It is intended to help God's people express themselves in worship in a way that is contemporary and heartfelt, yet rooted in scripture and tradition. Two hundred years ago, hymn writers and composers were quite innovative. They used not only scripture quotations and paraphrases, but also commentary on scripture. Many of the texts in this book go back over two hundred years, returning to scripture itself as source of the lyrics. The timeless message expresses itself in this book through up-to-date music.

**Why This Volume?** The *Chorus Book* comes in this Words and Music Edition. It contains not only words and music, but also chord symbols for each song, making this edition helpful for guitarists and other contemporary musicians.

**Indexes.** The extensive indexes in this Words and Music Edition of the *Chorus Book* and the ones in your hymnal can help you put together effective worship medleys. The indexes can also help you find choruses for various places in your order of worship.

## How to Begin

Before starting to use this collection, take some time to discover some things about your congregation. By looking at past bulletins and taking official or unofficial surveys, find out what your people like to sing. Notice whether any particular styles stand out as favorites. Perhaps your congregation already prefers hymns and songs that sound contemporary. These songs and hymns can serve as a bridge to using the selections in this volume.

Also, take the time to sing each chorus in the *Chorus Book*. Have an accompanist and singer help you as needed. Make note of songs and choruses that would blend well with the music your congregation already loves. Some of the choruses fit well with classic hymns, some with gospel songs, and some blend better with other contemporary hymns.

You will notice some traditional hymns and refrains in the *Chorus Book*. Hymns have an important place even in contemporary worship. If your congregation has been singing choruses exclusively, the hymns and refrains in this collection will be a good bridge back to classic hymnody; we still can learn much from the wisdom in traditional hymns.

## Start with the Familiar

**In Worship Patterns.** You do not need to significantly change your existing order of worship as you begin to use the *Chorus Book*. You will find calls to worship, songs of praise, baptism, holy communion, and healing, various responses, and closing songs, which will, therefore, fit well into an historic pattern for worship. In this pattern, we gather as God's people, receive the Word of God, share in the sacraments, and are sent forth to be God's people in the world. The songs contained in this collection will thus help contemporary worshipers feel connected with one another, with God, and with the church of all ages.

Choruses not only fit into familiar orders of worship, but also can actually help the flow of worship. Here are some examples of choruses in various spots:

| | | |
|---|---|---|
| Call to Worship | "This Is the Day" | No. 11 |
| Entrance | "I Love You, Lord" | No. 12 |
| Call to Prayer | "Give Thanks" | No. 62 |
| Confession | "Create in Me a Clean Heart" | No. 50 |
| Offering | "For the Gift of Creation" | No. 63 |
| Dismissal | "Lord, Be Glorified" | No. 57 |

**Build Medleys.** It is helpful to include choruses in a medley with familiar and well-loved hymns, organized around a related scripture passage or theme. For instance, if your theme is "God's Holiness," you might join the hymn "Holy, Holy, Holy" (No. 13 herein, as well as in many popular hymnals), with the chorus "Holy Ground" (No. 5), and/or "Holy, Holy" (No. 10). Using Lamentations 2:22-23 as a theme, the chorus "The Steadfast Love of the Lord" (No. 26) leads beautifully into the hymn "Great Is Thy Faithfulness."

You can also use the Index of Musical Keys to build worship medleys. Picking songs in the same key or related keys will eliminate complicated key changes between songs, helping both instrumentalists and singers. Some congregations enjoy singing for fifteen minutes or more to begin their worship service. The following is an example of an opening medley using choruses and hymns from the *Chorus Book*.

| KEY | SONG TITLE | LOCATION |
|---|---|---|
| D | "We Bring the Sacrifice of Praise" | No. 3 |
| D | "I Will Call Upon the Lord" | No. 9 |
| D | "This Is the Day" | No. 11 |
| D | "Holy, Holy, Holy" | No. 13 |
| G | "Sweet, Sweet Spirit" | No. 7 |
| G | "We Worship and Adore You" | No. 6 |

Notice the flow and function of these songs (each of which may be repeated several times). In the first three songs we ask God to work within us during our worship and then call ourselves and the congregation to worship. In the next three songs we turn our attention from ourselves to God, from singing about God to singing to God. These songs in this order express our belief in and love for the Trinity.

You may need to order songs in such a way that you have several key changes. If so, the instrumentalists will need to work out any transpositions or tempo changes ahead of time. Your church music supplier can help you find books of transpositions for this purpose.

One final word about medleys: be sensitive to your congregation's need to sit or stand during the medley, especially if it is a long one. Invite the people to stand—don't command them. In this way you show respect for persons who find it difficult or impossible to stand. Go over your medley ahead of time and make note of the most appropriate times to sit or stand.

## Accompaniment and Leadership

While many of these choruses work well in combination with traditional hymns, quite often the traditional hymnlike "organ and piano" accompaniment simply doesn't work. Furthermore, not every classically trained musician feels comfortable playing contemporary choruses; they may wish to receive training in contemporary performance practices. Likewise, there may already be "band" musicians in your congregation who would like to accompany these choruses. In either case, the accompaniment can make or break your congregational singing.

**How Many Instruments?** Let three considerations guide your decision: First, the size of your congregation and the room you worship in. For fifteen worshipers in a large living room, one or two guitars, or a piano or electronic keyboard, is sufficient. For a congregation of a hundred in a worship center or sanctuary, one or two instruments will be fine if amplified by a good sound system, but a "praise band" with several instruments may be even better. You could include bass guitar, tambourine, and drums (if your congregation is ready for drums). If you have several hundred worshipers, the sky is the limit—use as many players as are available, considering the amount of available space for musicians.

The second consideration is the availability of contemporary musicians. If you don't have a band, one or two players will be fine. Quality is much more important than quantity.

Third, what will your congregation accept? If they are used to organ only or organ and piano, add new instruments slowly. Adding electric guitar, drums, bass, and synthesizer too quickly may evoke a negative reaction. Be sensitive to the congregation's state of readiness. Invite them to worship in this new way—and don't start by selling the pipe organ!

Finally, adequate rehearsal is imperative! It is far better to have one guitar or a piano played well than to have a full orchestra or band play out of tune and unprepared.

**Prerecorded Accompaniment.** If you have no instrumentalists available, take heart. For most of the songs in the *Chorus Book,* prerecorded accompaniment is available in several formats: cassette tapes, CDs, electronic hymnals, and MIDI files. Check with your local Christian music supplier or with individual publishers to find available accompaniment tracks. To use them, you need only a tape player or a CD player, a sound system, and the proper cords to connect them.

**MIDI (Musical Instrument Digital Interface)** files come on floppy disks. To use them you will need a MIDI file player or a multitimbral, MIDI-compatible electronic keyboard. MIDI files allow you to select the desired key, tempo, and instrumentation (from solo instrument to full orchestra). Your local musical instrument store can help you locate MIDI files and instruments and other related products and services.

**Sound Systems.** It is especially important to have high quality sound reproduction for contemporary music, and perhaps even more important to have a qualified sound system operator. If you have no such person currently available, many stores and sound contractors periodically have seminars for church sound technicians; and if you buy a sound system, chances are that the store will provide this training free of charge.

## What Is Your Role?

As the one bringing this *Chorus Book* into your worship, you can do several things to help your congregation. First, demonstrate strong leadership by preparing well: Know your congregation, their likes and potential dislikes; and know the contents of this book and the ways it can help your worship. Communicate this to your congregation with honest enthusiasm.

Next, make sure you have good instrumentation and sound, whether you use one or two acoustic instruments or a full orchestra and a large sound system. Although quantity of instruments and volume should fit the size of your congregation and meeting place, quality should be of primary importance.

Finally, have someone with a pleasant singing voice to lead the congregation. Although the organ or piano may lead traditional hymns, a strong vocal leader is much more appropriate leading contemporary choruses, not with hand and arm movement, but with a clear, confident voice.

**Other Resources.** Slides and overhead transparencies are available for projecting the lyrics onto screens or blank walls. Christian Copyright Licensing, Inc. (CCLI) sells a church license to use thousands of Christian songs, hymns, and choruses in your church's worship. Contact CCLI at (800) 234-2446.

**Worship Magazines.** Ecumenical worship magazines are an excellent source of ideas and providers of products and services for contemporary worship and music. Two leading magazines are *Psalmist Magazine* (314) 532-7711, and *Worship Leader Magazine* (615) 386-3011.

Worship joyfully! May God guide and empower us all as we seek to worship in spirit and in truth. *Soli Deo gloria.*

# Call to Worship

*Music for the gathering of God's people*

## Surely the Presence of the Lord

*(Genesis 28:16 [Acts 2:1-4])*

1

WORDS: Lanny Wolfe
MUSIC: Lanny Wolfe

# Arise, Shine

### (Isaiah 60:1 [Matthew 5:16])

WORDS: Isaiah 60:1
MUSIC: Gary Alan Smith

# We Bring the Sacrifice of Praise

*(Hebrews 13:15; Psalm 50:14, 23; 107:22; 116:17; Jonah 2:9)*

WORDS and MUSIC: Kirk Dearman

# From the Rising of the Sun

*(Psalm 35:28; 113:3; Malachi 1:11 [Psalm 71:8])*

From the ris-ing of the sun ___ to the go-ing down of the same, ___ the name of the Lord shall be praised. ___ From the ris-ing of the sun ___ to the go-ing down of the same, ___ the

WORDS and MUSIC: Anon.

# Holy Ground

*(Exodus 3:5; Acts 7:33 [Revelation 7:11])*

WORDS and MUSIC: Geron Davis

# We Worship and Adore You

*(Matthew 2:11; Revelation 5:14)*

WORDS: Traditional
MUSIC: Trad.; arr. by Nylea L. Butler-Moore

# 7

# Sweet, Sweet Spirit

(Acts 2:1-4)

With an easy gospel feel (♩ = 92)

WORDS and MUSIC: Doris Akers

love; and for these bless-ings we lift our hearts in praise; with-out a

doubt we'll know that we have been re-vived when we shall leave this place. _____

## Alleluia

8

*(Revelation 19:1, 6)*

1. Al - le - lu - ia, al - le - lu - ia, al - le - lu - ia, al - le -

lu - ia, al - le - lu - ia, al - le - lu - ia, al - le - lu - ia, al - le - lu - ia.

2. He's my Savior.
3. I will praise him.
4. Blessed Jesus.
5. Precious Savior.
6. My Redeemer.
7. Lord, we love you.

8. Are we ready? *(Advent)*
9. Infant Savior. *(Christmas)*
10. We have seen him. *(Epiphany)*
11. He is risen! *(Easter)*
12. Feel the Spirit. *(Pentecost)*
13. He will wash us. *(Baptism)*
14. He will feed us. *(Holy Communion)*

WORDS: St. 1-3 by Jerry Sinclair; st. 4-7 anon.; st. 8-12 by Andy Langford; st. 13-14 by Gary Alan Smith
MUSIC: Jerry Sinclair

# I Will Call upon the Lord

*(2 Samuel 22:47; Psalm 18:3, 46 [Psalm 144:1])*

WORDS and MUSIC: Michael O'Shields

# Holy, Holy

### 10

*(Isaiah 6:3; Revelation 4:8 [Matthew 5:45; Galatians 4:6; 1 John 2:1; 3:1])*

1. Ho - ly, ho - ly, ho - ly, ho - ly, ho - ly, we're so ho - ly, Lord God Al - might - y: and we lift our hands be - fore you as a to - ken of our love, ho - ly, ho - ly, ho - ly, ho - ly.
2. Gra - cious Fa - ther, gra - cious Fa - ther, we're so blest to be your chil - dren, gra - cious Fa - ther; gra - cious Fa - ther, gra - cious Fa - ther.
3. Pre - cious Je - sus, pre - cious Je - sus, come and glad that you've re - deemed us, pre - cious Je - sus; pre - cious Je - sus, pre - cious Je - sus.
4. Ho - ly Spir - it, Ho - ly Spir - it, come and fill our hearts a - new, Ho - ly Spir - it; Ho - ly Spir - it, Ho - ly Spir - it.
5. Hal - le - lu - jah, hal - le - lu - jah, hal - le - lu - jah, hal - le - lu - jah; hal - le - lu - jah, hal - le - lu - jah.

WORDS and MUSIC: Jimmy Owens
© 1972 by Bud John Songs, Inc. Admin. by EMI Christian Music Publishing.

## 11
# This Is the Day
### (Psalm 118:24)

WORDS: Based on Psalm 118:24; adapt. by Les Garrett
MUSIC: Les Garrett

# Praise

*Praise to God, our Creator, Redeemer, Sustainer, and Friend*

## I Love You, Lord

12

*(Psalm 18:1; 35:9; 116:1-2 [2 Chronicles 6:40; Psalm 31:23])*

WORDS and MUSIC: Laurie Klein

# 13

# Holy, Holy, Holy

*(Isaiah 6:3; Revelation 4:6-11; 5:8 [8:3-4])*

WORDS: Reginald Heber
MUSIC: John B. Dykes; arr. by Nylea L. Butler-Moore
Arr. © 1995 Abingdon Press

# Sing unto the Lord a New Song

(Psalm 96:1; Isaiah 42:10 [Psalm 33:3; 98:1; 144:9; 149:1; Revelation 14:3])

**14**

WORDS: Jewish folk song
MUSIC: Jewish folk song; arr. by J. Michael Bryan
Arr. © 1996 Abingdon Press

## 15

# Awesome God

*(Deuteronomy 10:17; Psalm 33:8; Revelation 5:12*
*[Matthew 13:54; Mark 6:2; Revelation 7:12; 19:6-7])*

WORDS and MUSIC: Rich Mullins
© 1988 BMG Songs, Inc.

## 16

# Blessed Be the Name

*(Ruth 4:14; Nehemiah 9:5; Job 1:21; Psalm 72:19; 113:2*
*[Psalm 96:2; 100:4; 103:1; 145:1, 21])*

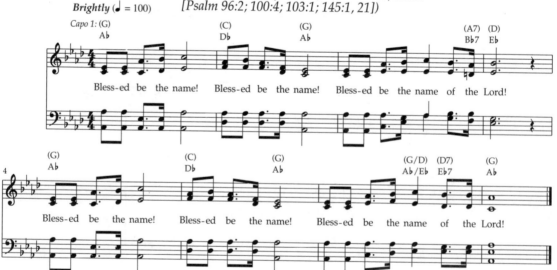

WORDS: USA campmeeting chorus
MUSIC: USA campmeeting melody; arr. by Ralph E. Hudson

# We Will Glorify

## 17

*(Deuteronomy 4:39; John 3:31; Revelation 5:13-14)*

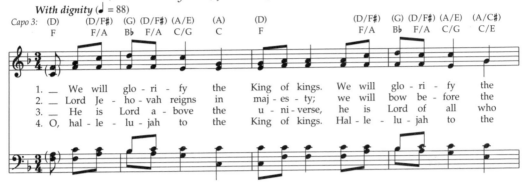

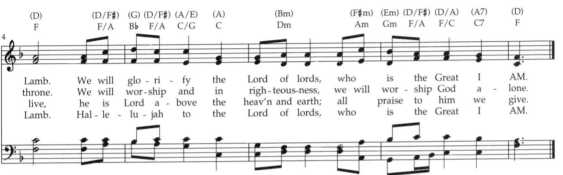

1. _ We will glo-ri-fy the King of kings. We will glo-ri-fy the
2. _ Lord Je-ho-vah reigns in maj-es-ty; we will bow be-fore the
3. _ He is Lord a-bove the u-ni-verse, he is Lord of all who
4. O, hal-le-lu-jah to the King of kings. Hal-le-lu-jah to the

Lamb. We will glo-ri-fy the Lord of lords, who is the Great I AM.
throne. We will wor-ship and in righ-teous-ness, we will wor-ship God a-lone.
live, he is Lord a-bove the heav'n and earth; all praise to him we give.
Lamb. Hal-le-lu-jah to the Lord of lords, who is the Great I AM.

WORDS and MUSIC: Twila Paris

# Praise the Lord

## 18

*(Psalm 148:1-2)*

Praise the Lord our God, praise the Lord! Praise him from the heights, praise the

Lord. Praise him an-gel throngs, praise the Lord. Praise God, praise the Lord!

WORDS: Richard Bewes
MUSIC: African American spiritual; harm. by Carlton R. Young

# 19 How Majestic Is Your Name

*(Psalm 8:1,9; Isaiah 9:6; Philippians 2:9)*

# I'm Goin'a Sing When the Spirit Says Sing     20
### (1 Corinthians 2:12; 12:4-11; 14:15)

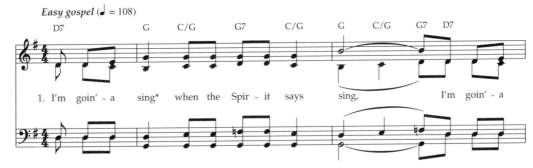

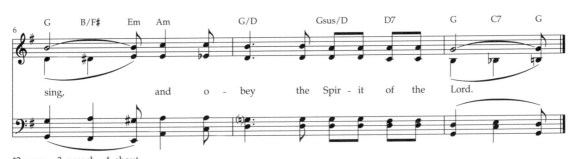

*2. pray    3. preach    4. shout

WORDS: African American spiritual
MUSIC: African American spiritual, adapt. by William Farley Smith
Adapt. © 1989 The United Methodist Publishing House

# 21

# You Are

*(Genesis 1:2-3; John 3:8)*

WORDS: Mike Graham
MUSIC: Cathy Townley; arr. by Henry Wiens; arr. adapt. by Nylea L. Butler-Moore

## 22

# Hosanna

*(Psalm 34:3; Isaiah 25:1; Matthew 21:9; Mark 11:9-10; John 12:13; Revelation 17:14; 19:16)*

WORDS: Carl Tuttle
MUSIC: Carl Tuttle; arr. by Joseph Linn

## More Precious than Silver

*(Psalm 119:72)*

23

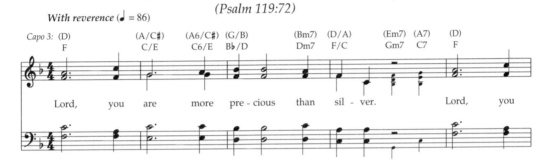

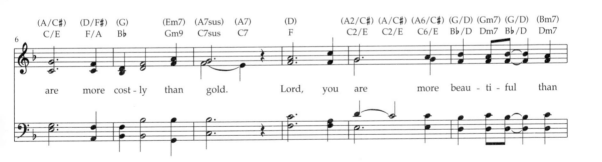

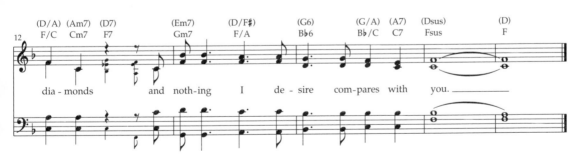

WORDS and MUSIC: Lynn DeShazo

## 24 Your Loving Kindness Is Better than Life

*(Psalm 63:3-4)*

WORDS: Based on Psalm 63:3, 4
MUSIC: Hugh Mitchell

bless you. I will lift up my hands un-to your name. Your lov-ing
(We) (our)

## Bless the Lord, O My Soul  25

*(Psalm 103:1)*

Bless the Lord, O my soul; bless the

Lord, O my soul; and all that is with-

in me bless his ho - ly name.

WORDS: Anon.
MUSIC: Anon.; arr. by J. Michael Bryan
Arr. © 1996 Abingdon Press

## 26      The Steadfast Love of the Lord

*(Lamentations 3:22-23)*

WORDS: Edith McNeill
MUSIC: Edith McNeill; arr. by J. Michael Bryan

# Praise Jesus

*Praise to Jesus our Savior*

## All Hail King Jesus

*(Matthew 21:9; Mark 11:9-10; John 12:13)*

WORDS and MUSIC: Dave Moody

# 28

# He Is Exalted
## (Ele é exaltado)

*Gentle Rock* (♩. = 60)  *(Psalm 47:9; Acts 5:31; Philippians 2:9)*

He is ex-alt-ed, the King is ex-alt-ed on high. I will
Ele é ex-al-ta-do, O senhor é ex-al-ta-do no céu Eu o

praise him. He is ex-alt-ed, for-ev-er ex-alt-ed, and I will
lou-vo. Ele é ex-al-ta-do, O sen-hor é ex-al-ta-do no céu Céu

praise his name! He is the Lord. For-
lou-var-ei! Ele é o sen-hor. E

ev-er his truth shall reign. Heav-en and earth re-joice in this ho-ly
pra sem-pre rei-na-ra. Ter-ra e céu Se a-le-gram em le a-do-

namé. He is ex-alt-ed, the King is ex-alt-ed on high.
rar. Ele é ex-al-ta-do, O sen-hor é ex-al-ta-do no céu.

*Second time through, "He is" can be changed to "You are" or "Christ is," etc.*

WORDS: Twila Paris; Portuguese trans. anon.
MUSIC: Twila Paris; arr. by Nylea L. Butler-Moore

# Emmanuel, Emmanuel

*(Isaiah 7:14; Matthew 1:23)*

WORDS and MUSIC: Bob McGee

# 30 His Name Is Wonderful
## (Maravilloso es)
### (Isaiah 9:6)

WORDS: Audrey Mieir; Spanish trans. by Marjorie J. de Caudill
MUSIC: Audrey Mieir

# Our God Reigns

*(Isaiah 52:7; 53:2-6, 12; Romans 10:15; Revelation 19:6)*

1. How love-ly on the moun-tains are the feet of him who brings good news, good news an-nounc-ing peace, pro-claim-ing news of hap-pi-ness: Our God reigns! Our God reigns! Our God reigns! Our God reigns! Our God reigns!

2. He had no state-ly form; he had no maj-es-ty that we should be drawn to him. He was de-spised, and we took no ac-count of him; yet now he reigns with the Most High! Our God reigns!

3. It was our sin and guilt that bruised and wound-ed him. It was our sin that brought him down. When we like sheep had gone a-stray, our Shep-herd came and on his shoul-ders bore our shame.

4. Out of the tomb he came with grace and maj-es-ty. He is a-live! He is a-live! God loves us so — see here his hands, his feet, his side. Yes we know he is a-live!

WORDS and MUSIC: Leonard E. Smith, Jr.

## 32  I Exalt You

*(Exodus 15:2; Psalm 97:9; Isaiah 25:1)*

WORDS: Pete Sanchez, Jr.
MUSIC: Pete Sanchez, Jr.; arr. by J. Michael Bryan

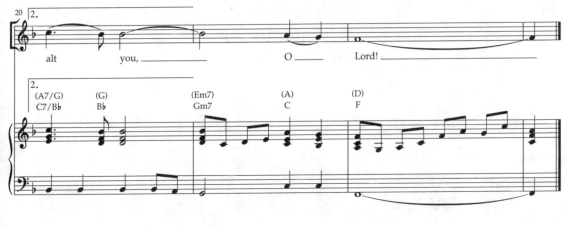

# Jesus, Name Above All Names

**33**

*(Philippians 2:9-11)*

1. Je - sus, Name a - bove all names, beau - ti - ful Sav - ior, glo - ri - ous Lord. Em - man - u - el, God is with us, bless - ed Re - deem - er, liv - ing Word.

2. I AM, Light of the Gen - tiles, Lord God Al - might - y, Prince of Peace. El Shad - dai; God is Suf - fi - cient, Shep - herd of Souls, King of kings.

3. Lil - y of the Val - ley, Son of Da - vid, Rose of Sha - ron, the Al - pha and O - me - ga, Seed of Jes - se, Morn - ing Star.

4. Je - sus, our In - ter - ces - sor, prom - ised Mes - si - ah, Bread of Life, the Giv - er of Liv - ing Wa - ter, might - y Bap - tiz - er, Son of God.

WORDS: St. 1 by Naida Hearn; sts. 2-4 anonymous
MUSIC: Naida Hearn

# 34

# Majesty
# (¡Majestad!)

*(Psalm 96:6; Jude 25; Revelation 4:11)*

WORDS: Jack Hayford; Spanish trans. J. Alfonso Lockward
MUSIC: Jack Hayford

## 35

# O How He Loves You and Me!

*(John 3:16; Romans 5:8; Galatians 2:20; Ephesians 5:2)*

1. O how he loves you and me; \_\_\_\_\_ O how he loves you and me. \_\_\_\_\_ He gave his life, what more could he give? O how he loves you, O how he loves me, O how he loves you and me! \_\_\_\_\_

2. Je - sus to Cal - vary did go, \_\_\_\_\_ his love for peo - ple to show. \_\_\_\_\_ What he did there brought hope from de - spair: O how he loves you, O how he loves me, O how he loves you and me! \_\_\_\_\_

WORDS and MUSIC: Kurt Kaiser
© 1975 Word Music

## 36

# Praise the Name of Jesus

*(2 Samuel 22:2-3; Psalm 18:2; 144:2)*

Praise the name of Je - sus. Praise the name of Je - sus. He's my Rock, *(our)* he's my For - tress, *(our)* He's my De - liv - er - er; in *(our)*

WORDS and MUSIC: Roy Hicks, Jr.
© 1976 Latter Rain Music

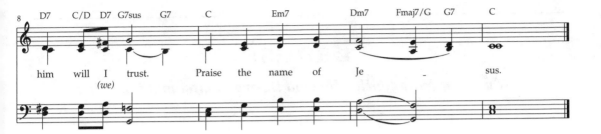

him will I trust. Praise the name of Je - sus.
*(we)*

## There's Something About That Name 37
### (Es Jesús nombre sin par)

**Easy gospel** (♩ = 96)  *(Psalm 135:13; Philippians 2:9-11)*

Je - sus, Je - sus, Je - sus! There's just some-thing a - bout that name!
Cris - to, Je - su - cris - to es un nom - bre sin i - gual.

Mas - ter, Sav - ior, Je - sus! Like the fra-grance af - ter the rain.
Ver - bo, Dios es Cris - to, co-mo o - lor a llu - via es El.

Je - sus, Je - sus, Je - sus! Let all heav-en and earth pro - claim:
Cris - to, Je - su - cris - to, cie-lo y tie - rra glo - ria den.

Kings and king-doms will all pass a - way, but there's some-thing a - bout that name!
Re - yes, rei - nos al fin pa - sa - rán, mas su nom - bre es e - ter - nal.

WORDS: Gloria Gaither and William J. Gaither; Spanish trans. by Pedro P. Pirón
MUSIC: William J. Gaither

# Baptism

*Music for our adoption by God through water and the Spirit*

**38**

# Come, Be Baptized

*(Matthew 28:19; Acts 2:38-39)*

*Performance Options*

    Accompanied — As written (piano and/or guitar). May be sung in unison or parts.

    Accompanied — Begin at measure 5; play voice parts and cue-sized notes; end at measure 19. May be sung in unison or parts.

    Unaccompanied — Begin at measure 5; end at measure 19. Sing in parts.

WORDS and MUSIC: Gary Alan Smith

# 39

# Only by Grace

*(Ephesians 2:4-18; 2 Timothy 1:9)*

WORDS and MUSIC: Gerrit Gustafson

## 40

# We Are One in Christ Jesus
## (Somos uno en Cristo)

*(Ephesians 4:4-6)*

*With great enthusiasn (♩ = 120)*

We are one in Christ Je - sus, all one bod - y, all one spir - it, all to -
*So - mos u - no en Cris - to, so - mos u - no, so - mos u - no, u - no.*

geth - er. We are geth - er. We share one God, one might - y
*só - lo. So - mos só - lo. Un so - lo Dios, un so - lo Se -*

Lord, one a - bid - ing faith, one bind - ing love, one sin - gle bap -
*ñor, u - na so - la fe, un so - lo a - mor, un so - lo bau -*

ti - sm, one Ho - ly Com - fort - er, the Ho - ly Spir - it, u - nit - ing all.
*tis - mo, un so - lo Es - pí - ri - tu y e - se es el Con - so - la - dor.*

WORDS: Anon.; English trans. by Alice Parker
MUSIC: Anon.; arr. by Felipe Blycker J.

Trans. © 1996 Abingdon Press; arr. © 1992 Celebremos/Libros Alianza

# Holy Communion

*Music for taking, blessing, breaking, and giving the holy meal*

## Let Us Break Bread Together

41

*(1 Corinthians 10:16-17; 11:25-32)*

1. Let us break bread to-geth-er on our knees; _____ let us
2. Let us drink wine to-geth-er on our knees; _____ let us
3. Let us praise God to-geth-er on our knees; _____ let us

break bread to-geth-er on our knees. _____
drink wine to-geth-er on our knees. _____  } When I fall on my knees with my
praise God to-geth-er on our knees. _____

face to the ris-ing sun, O Lord, have mer-cy on me. _____

WORDS: African American spiritual
MUSIC: African American spiritual; harm. by Carlton R. Young
Harm. © 1965 Abingdon Press

## 42

# Fill My Cup, Lord

(John 4:5-15; 6:35, 48)

Fill my cup, Lord, I lift it up, Lord! Come and quench this thirst-ing of my soul. Bread of heav-en, feed me till I want no more; fill my cup, fill it up and make me whole!

WORDS and MUSIC: Richard Blanchard
© 1959 Richard Blanchard and © 1964 Sacred Songs

## 43

# Eat This Bread

(Luke 22:19-20; John 6:35, 48)

Eat this bread, drink this cup, come to me and nev-er be hun-gry.
Eat this bread, drink this cup, trust in me and you will not thirst.

WORDS: Robert Batastini and the Taizé Community
MUSIC: Jacques Berthier
© 1984 Les Presses de Taizé France; by permission of G.I.A. Publications, Inc.

# One Bread, One Body

## (1 Corinthians 10:16-17; 12:12-13, 20; Ephesians 4:4-6)

WORDS: John B. Foley
MUSIC: John B. Foley; arr. by J. Michael Bryan

## 45

# Take Our Bread

*(Luke 22:19-20)*

WORDS: Joe Wise
MUSIC: Joe Wise; arr. by J. Michael Bryan

# Healing

***Music for wholenesss of body, mind, relationships, and spirit***

## Through It All 46

*(Job 19:25; 1 Timothy 4:10; 1 Peter 1:21)*

***Gospel style*** (♩ = 88)

Capo 3: (D) Eb (D7) Eb7 (G) Ab (Em) Fm7
Through it all, through it all, I've
(A) Bb (A7) Bb7 (D) Eb (A7) Bb7 (D) Eb
learned to trust in Je - sus, I've learned to trust in God;
(D7) Eb7 (G) Ab (Em) Fm
through it all, through it all, I've
(A) Bb (A7) Bb7 (D) Eb (G/D) Ab/Eb (D) Eb
learned to de - pend up - on God's word.


WORDS and MUSIC: Andraé Crouch

47

# Spirit Song

*(Acts 2:4; 4:31; Romans 15:13)*

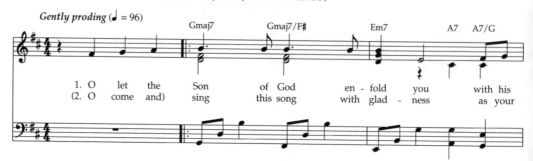

1. O let the Son of God en-fold you with his
(2. O come and) sing this song with glad - ness as your

Spir - it and his love. Let him fill your heart and
hearts are filled with joy. Lift your hands in sweet sur -

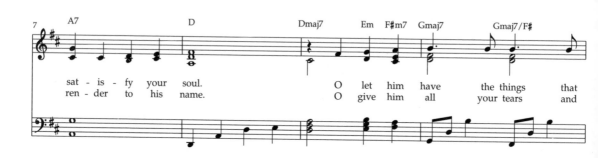

sat - is - fy your soul. O let him have the things that
ren - der to his name. O give him all your tears and

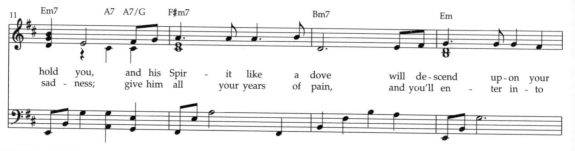

hold you, and his Spir - it like a dove will de - scend up - on your
sad - ness; give him all your years of pain, and you'll en - ter in - to

WORDS and MUSIC: John Wimber

**48**

# People Need the Lord

*(John 10:7, 9)*

*With an easy beat* (♩ = 92)

Peo-ple need the Lord, — peo-ple need the Lord.

At the end of bro-ken dreams, — he's the o-pen door. —

Peo-ple need the Lord, — peo-ple need the Lord. —

When will we re-al-ize peo-ple need the Lord.

WORDS: Greg Nelson and Phil McHugh
MUSIC: Greg Nelson and Phil McHugh; arr. by J. Michael Bryan

# All I Need Is You

49

*(Psalm 84; 1 Corinthians 1:30)*

WORDS and MUSIC: Dan Adler; arr. by Nylea L. Butler-Moore

# 50 Create in Me a Clean Heart

*(Psalm 51:10)*

Create in me a clean heart, O God,
*(us)*
and renew a right spirit within me.
*(us.)*
Cre-
Cast me not away from your presence, O
*(us)*
Lord, and take not your Holy Spirit from me.
*(us.)*

WORDS: Anon.
MUSIC: Anon.; arr. by J. Michael Bryan
Arr. © 1996 Abingdon Press

## Turn Your Eyes upon Jesus

51

*(Revelation 22:4)*

WORDS and MUSIC: Helen Lemmel

# 52 Change My Heart, O God

*(Psalm 51:10; Isaiah 64:8; Jeremiah 31:33)*

# Spirit of the Living God

**53**

(Acts 2:4; 2 Corinthians 3:3)

*Prayerfully* (♩ = 72)

WORDS and MUSIC: Daniel Iverson

# 54

# You Are Mine

*(Isaiah 43:1)*

With quiet confidence (♩ = 84)

Do not be a-fraid, I am with you. I have called you each by name. Come and fol-low me, I will bring you home. I love you and you are mine.

# Unity 55

*(Psalm 133:1; Ephesians 4:3)*

WORDS: Tim Reynolds
MUSIC: Tim Reynolds; arr. by J. Michael Bryan
Arr. © 1996 Abingdon Press

# 56     God, You Are My God

(*Psalm 31:14; 63:1, 4; 118:28; 119:1, 3; 143:10; Isaiah 25:1*)

WORDS and MUSIC: Rich Mullins and Beaker

# Responses to the Word

### Music as response to God's Word read and proclaimed

**57**

# Lord, Be Glorified

*(John 15:8; 1 Corinthians 6:20; 2 Corinthians 9:13; 2 Thessalonians 1:11-20)*

WORDS: Sts. 1-3 by Bob Kilpatrick; sts. 4-6 by J. Michael Bryan, Anne Burnette, Andy Langford, Brian McSwain
MUSIC: Bob Kilpatrick

# Kum Ba Yah

*(Psalm 141:1; 1 Corinthians 6:22b)*

WORDS: African American spiritual
MUSIC: African American spiritual; arr. by Ken Moore

Arr. © 1996 Abingdon Press

**59**

# Our Love Belongs to You, O Lord
## (Amarte sólo a ti, Señor)

*(Psalm 62:12; 143:10; Isaiah 40:31; 1 Peter 1:21)*

WORDS: Anon.; English trans. by George Lockwood
MUSIC: Anon.; arr. by Jorge Lockward

English trans. and arr. © 1996 Abingdon Press

# 60 Great Is the Lord

*(Psalm 111:7; 118:3; 145:3; Revelation 4:11; 5:12; 19:11)*

WORDS and MUSIC: Michael W. Smith and Deborah D. Smith

# Jesu, Jesu

*(John 13:5-17)*

61

WORDS: Tom Colvin
MUSIC: Ghana folk song; arr. by Tom Colvin; harm. by Charles H. Webb

# 62 Give Thanks

*(1 Samuel 2:4-8; Luke 1:51-53; 2 Corinthians 9:15; Colossians 3:15-17)*

WORDS and MUSIC: Henry Smith

# For the Gift of Creation

(Deuteronomy 26:10)

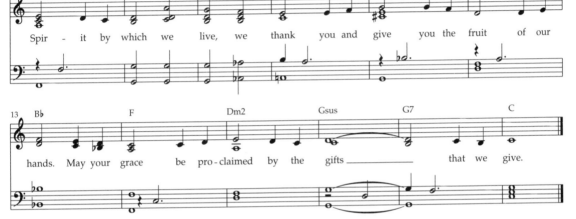

For the gift of cre-a-tion, the gift of your love, and the gift of the Spir-it by which we live, we thank you and give you the fruit of our hands. May your grace be pro-claimed by the gifts _____ that we give.

WORDS and MUSIC: Steve Garnass-Holmes
© 1992 Abingdon Press

# Jesus, Remember Me

(Luke 23:42)

Je-sus, re-mem-ber me when you come in-to your king-dom.

Je-sus, re-mem-ber me when you come in-to your king-dom.

WORDS: Based on Luke 23:42
MUSIC: Jacques Berthier and the Taizé Community
Music © 1981 Les Presses de Taizé, by permission of G.I.A. Publications, Inc.

# 65

# I Call You Faithful

*(Matthew 1:21; Luke 1:31; 2:21; 1 Corinthians 1:9; Revelation 19:11)*

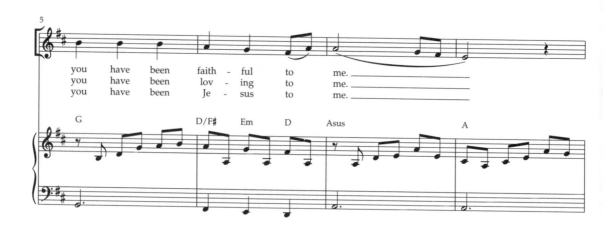

WORDS: Bobby Price
MUSIC: Kevin Walker; arr. by J. Michael Bryan

# Ubi Caritas
## (Live in Charity)
*(John 15:9-11; 1 John 4:12, 16)*

faith - ful you are, and faith - ful you'll be. \_\_\_\_
lov - ing you are, and lov - ing you'll be. \_\_\_\_
Je - sus you are, and Je - sus you'll

be. \_\_\_\_

U - bi ca - ri - tas et a -
*Live in char - i - ty and stead - fast*

mor, u - bi ca - ri - tas De - us i bi est.
*love. Live in char - i - ty. God will dwell with you.*

WORDS and MUSIC: Jacques Berthier and the Taizé Community; arr. by J. Michael Bryan
© 1979, 1996 Les Presses de Taizé, by permission of G.I.A. Publications, Inc.

## 67

# Saranam, Saranam
## (Refuge)

*(Psalm 18:2, 61:1-4; 91:1-2)*

*Gently flowing* (♩ = 78)

Je - sus, Sav - ior, Lord, lo, to thee I fly:

Sar - a - nam, Sar - a - nam, Sar - a - nam;

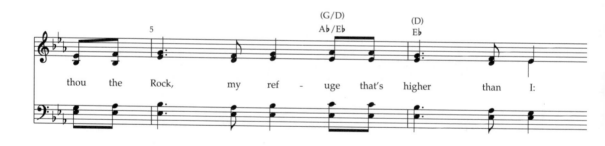

thou the Rock, my ref - uge that's higher than I:

Sar - a - nam, Sar - a - nam, Sar - a - nam.

WORDS: Trad. Pakistani; trans. by D. T. Niles
MUSIC: Trad. Punjabi melody; arr. by Shanti Rasanayagam
Trans. and arr. by permission of Christian Conference of Asia

# Learning to Lean

(2 Timothy 1:12)

*With a gospel feel* (♩ = 78)

Learn - ing to lean, learn - ing to lean, I'm
(we're)
learn - ing to lean on Je - sus; find - ing more power than
I'd ev - er dreamed, I'm learn - ing to lean on Je - sus.
(we'd) (We're)

WORDS and MUSIC: John Stallings

# God Is So Good

(Psalm 106:1; Matthew 6:10; Romans 10:9)

*Simply* (♩ = 88)

Capo 1: (D)

1. God is so good, God is so good,
2. God cares for me, God cares for me,
3. He is my Lord, he is my Lord,
4. I'll do God's will, I'll do God's will,

God is so good,
God cares for me,
he is my Lord,
I'll do God's will,
he's so good to me!
(God's)

WORDS and MUSIC: Anon.

# 70

# Refiner's Fire

*(Psalm 51:10; Malachi 3:2-3)*

WORDS and MUSIC: Brian Doerksen

## I Am Loved

71

*(John 13:34; 1 John 4:11)*

ho - ly, set a - part for you, _____ my Mas - ter,

read - y to do your will. _____

**Sweetly** (♩ = 96)

Capo 1: (D)

I am loved, I am loved, I can risk lov - ing you, for the
(You are) (you are) (you) (lov - ing, too,)

One who knows me best loves me most. _____ I am loved, you are loved — won't you
(you) (you) (we)

please take my hand? We are free to love each oth - er — we are loved. _____
(our)

WORDS: William J. Gaither and Gloria Gaither
MUSIC: William J. Gaither

# 72 Shine, Jesus, Shine

*(2 Corinthians 3:18; 4:6; Ephesians 5:14; Revelation 21:23-24)*

With energy (♩ = 120)

Shine, Je-sus, shine, _ fill this land with the Fa-ther's glo-ry, blaze, Spir-it, blaze, _ set our hearts on fire; flow, riv-er, flow _ _ flood the na-tions with grace and mer-cy, send forth your word, _ _ Lord, and let there be light.

1. Lord, the light of your
2. Lord, I come to your
3. As we gaze on your

1. love is shin-ing in the midst of the dark-ness shin-ing; Je-sus, Light of the
2. awe-some pres-ence from the shad-ows in-to your ra-di-ance; by the blood I may
3. king-ly bright-ness, so our fa-ces dis-play your like-ness; ev-er chang-ing from

WORDS and MUSIC: Graham Kendrick

World, shine up-on us, set us free by the truth you now bring us.
en-ter your bright-ness, search me, try me, con-sume all my dark-ness.
glo-ry to glo-ry, mir-rored here may our lives tell your sto-ry.

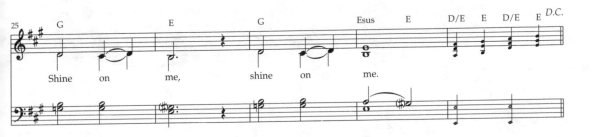

Shine on me, shine on me.

## He Is Lord
## (El es Rey)

73

*(Romans 10:9; Philippians 2:10-11)*

**Warmly** (♩ = 60)

He is Lord, he is Lord! He is ris - en from the dead and he is
El es Rey, es Se - ñor. Cris - to ya re-su-ci - tó y es Se -

Lord! Ev-ery knee shall bow, ev-ery tongue con - fess that Je - sus Christ is Lord.
ñor. De ro - di - llas to - dos hoy con - fe - se - mos: ¡El es el Se - ñor!

WORDS: Traditional; Spanish trans. by Felicia Fina
MUSIC: Traditional; arr. by Tom Fettke

Arr. © 1986 Word Music; Spanish trans. © 1996 Abingdon Press

**74**

# They'll Know We Are Christians
# by Our Love

*(1 Corinthians 12:12-13)*

*With quiet intensity* (♩ = 56)

Capo 1: (Em)
Fm

1. We are one in the Spir - it, we are one in the Lord. We are
2. We will walk with each oth - er, we will walk hand in hand. We will
3. We will work with each oth - er, we will work side by side. We will
4. All praise to the Fa - ther, from whom all things come, and all

one in the Spir - it, we are one in the Lord, and we pray that all
walk with each oth - er, we will walk hand in hand, and to - geth - er we'll
work with each oth - er, we will work side by side, and we'll guard each one's
praise to Christ Je - sus, his on - ly Son and all praise to the

u - ni - ty may one day be re - stored:
spread the news that God is in our land: And they'll know we are Chris - tians by our
dig - ni - ty and save each one's pride:
Spir - it, who makes us one:

love, by our love. Yes, they'll know we are Chris - tians by our love. _____

WORDS and MUSIC: Peter Scholtes

# Something Beautiful

*(John 8:10-12)*

Some-thing beau-ti-ful, some-thing good;
all my con-fu-sion he un-der-stood;
all I had to of-fer him was bro-ken-ness and
strife, but he made some-thing beau-ti-ful of my life.

WORDS: Gloria Gaither
MUSIC: William J. Gaither
© 1971 William J. Gaither

# We Are His Hands

*(1 Corinthians 12:27-31)*

WORDS: Mark Gersmehl
MUSIC: Mark Gersmehl; arr. by J. Michael Bryan

# Thank You, Lord

*(Psalm 118:21; Revelation 11:17)*

Thank you, Lord. Thank you, Lord.

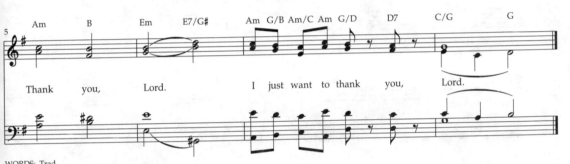

Thank you, Lord. I just want to thank you, Lord.

WORDS: Trad.
MUSIC: Trad.; adapt. and arr. by William Farley Smith
Adapt. and arr. © 1989 The United Methodist Publishing House

# Sanctuary

*(Romans 12:1; 1 Corinthians 3:16)*

Lord, pre-pare me to be a sanc-tu-ar-y, pure and ho-ly, tried and

true; with thanks-giv-ing, I'll be a liv-ing sanc-tu-ar-y for you.

WORDS and MUSIC: John Thompson and Randy Scruggs
© 1982 Whole Armor/Full Armor

# Walk with Me

(Psalm 86:11; John 8:12)

Walk with me, I will walk with you and (and)

build the land that God has planned where love shines through.

WORDS: John S. Rice
MUSIC: John S. Rice

# Thank You, Jesus
## (Tino tenda, Jesu)

(Psalm 118:21; Revelation 11:17; 19:4)

Thank you, Je - sus, a - men! Thank you, Je - sus, a - men! Thank you,
Ti - no ten - da, Je - su! Ti - no ten - da, Je - su! Ti - no

Je - sus, a - men! Al - le - lu - ia! A - men!
ten - da, Je - su! Ha - le - lu - jah! A - men!

WORDS: Original Shona language; trans. by Patrick Matsikenyiri
MUSIC: African folk song; transcription by Patrick Matsikenyiri; arr. by J. Michael Bryan

# My Tribute
## (To God Be the Glory)

*Majestically* (♩ = 76) *(Ephesians 1:6-7; Philippians 4:20; 1 Peter 1:2-3)*

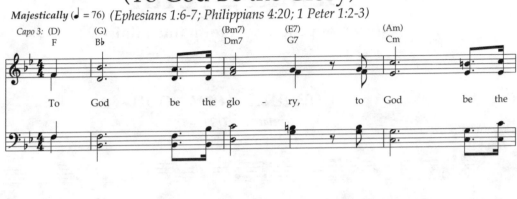

To God be the glo - ry, to God be the glo - ry, to God be the glo - ry for the things he has done. With his blood he has saved me; with his power he has raised me; to God be the glo - ry for the things he has done.

WORDS and MUSIC: Andraé Crouch

# Sending Forth

## Music for people sent forth into ministry

**82**

# Soon and Very Soon

*(Revelation 1:7; 21:3-4)*

*With enthusiasm (♩ = 108)*

1. Soon and ver - y soon, — we are going to see the King; —

(Hal - le - lu - jah!)

soon and ver - y soon, — we are going to see the King; —

(Hal - le - lu - jah!)

soon and ver - y soon, — we are going to see the King. — Hal - le -

lu - jah! Hal - le - lu - jah! We're going to see the King. —

2. No more dying there,
3. No more crying there,

WORDS: Andraé Crouch
MUSIC: Andraé Crouch; adapt. by William Farley Smith

# Doxology

*(Psalm 95:6; John 3:3-7; 8:12)*

WORDS and MUSIC: Steve Garnaas-Holmes
© 1992 Abingdon Press

# 84 Let Us Now Depart in Your Peace

*(Luke 2:29; Philippians 4:7-8)*

Let us now de-part in your peace, bless-ed Je-sus.

Send us to our homes with God's love in our hearts. __ Let not the bus-y world

claim all our loy-al-ties. Keep us ev-er mind-ful, dear Lord, of you.

A - men, a - men, a - men.

WORDS: New Mexican folk song; adapt. by Lee Hastings Bristol, Jr.
MUSIC: New Mexican folk song melody; harm. and arr. by Philip E. Baker

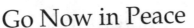

# Go Now in Peace

*(Luke 2:29; 2 Corinthians 13:11)*

85

Moderately (♩ = 56)

Go now in peace, go now in peace, may the love of

God sur - round you ev - ery-where, ev - ery-where you may go. go.

*Accompaniment may be keyboard, handbells, and/or Orff instruments*
*May be sung as a canon.*

WORDS and MUSIC: Natalie Sleeth
© 1976 Hinshaw Music, Inc. Reprinted by permission.

# On Eagle's Wings

*(Exodus 19:4; Matthew 13:43)*

86

Expressively (♩ = 86)

And God† will raise you* up on ea - gle's wings,

bear you* on the breath of dawn, make you* to shine like the sun, and

hold you* in the palm of God's‡ hand.

† or "you"
* or "us"
‡ or "your"

WORDS: Michael Joncas
MUSIC: Michael Joncas; harm. by Carlton R. Young
© 1979, 1991, New Dawn Music, 5536 NE Hassalo, Portland, OR 97213. All rights reserved. Used by permission.

# 87

# Shalom to You

(John 20:19-23; Philippians 4:7)

WORDS: Elise S. Eslinger
MUSIC: Trad. Spanish melody; harm. from *Celebremos*
Words © 1983 The United Methodist Publishing House

# May You Run and Not Be Weary

*(Isaiah 30:29; 40:31)*

WORDS and MUSIC: Paul Murakami and Handt Hanson; arr. by Henry Wiens; arr. adapt. by Nylea L. Butler-Moore
© 1991 Changing Church Forum

# INDEX OF COMPOSERS, ARRANGERS, AUTHORS, TRANSLATORS, AND SOURCES

# INDEX OF SCRIPTURE

# INDEX OF MUSICAL KEYS

# INDEX FOR THE CHRISTIAN YEAR

# INDEX OF TOPICS AND CATEGORIES

# INDEX OF FIRST LINES AND COMMON TITLES